Spiral Spill

chaos & clarity, visceral & tender

Maquel Kretschmer

BookLeaf Publishing

India | USA | UK

Made with ❤ on the BookLeaf Publishing Platform
www.bookleafpub.in
www.bookleafpub.com

Dedication

To all the selves that have carried me here.

Isa, my beloved
Lexi, my anchor
Callie, my right hand
Cara, my mirror

Preface

This is a collection of poetry written between where I was and where I wanted to be. This is my telling of how I found my footing and direction through collapse and introspection.

Where do you stand? What do you walk towards?

These poems are cornerstones of my journey of finding my authentic direction. They are reflections of what I have found at the bottom of myself.

Acknowledgements

To the earth that holds each of us, I keep finding myself to be a better friend to you.

this is my soft up

this is my feathering

willow

tree
roots to toes
ticking of heart
eternity of bones
the ruins of Willow
returning to terrain
grief and relief

there is a tree in my heart
i planted her there
to heal
from conditioned response
i go to her roots with open hands
with wails
with the continuous grief of consequences
& undoing
the digging out and tending
soil deep dark to knuckle
in this dance for willow

willow born from the throes of good girl woes
from belonging given,
reciprocity

fret cycles

the familiar lull of this self gaze
this worn alley of expression
this screen and these thumbs, these words within the
squares
a familiar pattern, rhythm emerges in the tapping
soothed

there's been some space between me and my gaze
with these words that shape a moment
grasp at some certainty i once was
ever changing
(cycles)

today I soothed and yelled
i nourished and raged—
fumed and cuddled
twenty minute spells of expression
releasing tension
for transition
for coming departure, leaving
i feel myself preparing to travel home
the warmth familiar
in the tingle at the parts of me that sometimes feel scared
home, a place where I do not fear

(that has not been here)

fret

and return to swirling center
i want to see the parts you want to hide
i want to walk towards them
make home in their wildness
that ache you can't tolerate is holy

beloved

sometimes
you may be the bird
and other times, the worm
today? It is neither,
(let down the filter)

today there is a hooded scythe
hunched over the back of your heart
and he is grinning the tricksters grin
tread with humor and courage
the path is fogged by design

sister

have you noticed?
the cleansing smoke
stirs the air
as your blood slips through the water
like the spider's web released
suspended, unfurling
you, the widening rose

you, the vessel
sister
you,

the pure, the wise, the perfect
and what I mean

can it be known?
the waver of our voices rising
the chorus

have you heard the children singing?
they are ours to tend

sister,

this is ours to tend, tender
tend her

and we will find home

grief garden

let's plant a grief garden
and tend it through the seasons
i reach through airwaves to press a dream of your
broken heart
you are a thousand miles away, and so are you and so are
you
so why not sow some seeds in the middle of a
thunderstorm
the dark of the night a cradle
watch the sky break forth with rain

women, gather

"i want to protect you."
and why shouldn't we?
women, gather
bring our backs together, draw the circle
say what you see from your side to the center

it is time for things to come undone
and the undone times will feel like hinges

seashells

love songs shared like sea shells
passing from ear to heart to belly
tiptoes through past corridors
brushing bare toes in sacred waters
interlocked and awake
distal, potent
memory a cloud of palo santo
memory the groove of redwood against back
kissing near water towers
i hear the waves calling
i shout back or maybe coo

home is a fickle lover
when she's drawn back on a winding road
with strangers turned lovers
scattered across the globe like
the rushing waters

all the rushing waters
they beckon
they steer us
back towards true north
towards more stars than mouth could count

a mouth, my mouth, yours
with lips and tongues and teeth
with words
drawing in closer to some ghost

some self passed
i am myself passing

where are you?

vertebral vertical

down below the bellows of the vertebral vertical
deep dark slip of selves layered to sludge
i drift and drop
meet and wind, twist become to bottom
where I stare

at every despicable face

and right here, tucked into the edges of
of joints and tissue
—the parts that resist, the parts that could never

even you,
i say, with love in my teeth gold
i hold something ferocious,
something reaching towards unthinkable
with my rolling eyes, my crooked smile

twisting back
i've grown myself one more neck
something fierce and resting
preparing, over extending, perhaps piercing
definitely reeling

i turn away my gaze
i turn
i

plunder is a release
a redistribution
a reckoning

trace the shape of an archetype
i'll show you my dark and light
heart tissue
express to you
with buds for hands
flowers

when I unwind I reach towards you twin
and as you contain
i draw in like a suspicious moth

light too bright to not chase
on a fierce summer night
lightning an entire world of road
eclipsed by trees
otherwise infinity sky
pure wise
all eyes
then mouth, fists, wheels

the furious wearies on the road
an hour in two directions split back
return to home
keep looping
like the nucleus

returning to center like a spiral
to be frank is nauseous
catch me in your whirligig, doc
this ride's turbulence

like a lance Iinked
bow pulled
breath becoming disappear reappear

becoming is for a feint heart
one pretending a direction
when love is infinity

beloved spiral and we get back
to the ocean

there is always tomorrow, yes, for certain,
version...

until.

....wide expanse...

harbor abyss

so much of me is a fight
when I want to be a port
a harbor but instead a plight
an ocean but the abyss yells
i am running
in circles
with thumbs and blue light

thirst

a virgin forest needs nothing else
interdependence
full of possibility
standing on its own

mother and virgin
the mother perceiving the virgin forest
the mother preparing
paving
pacing
perceiving
play and still
still like the forest
but yet still mothering
belonging to time or not
belonging to time or not
becoming the cycle I am within
being the now
forward forward

a women whole unto herself
creatrix and sustained
the vessel and the water, the bearer too
and why not the thirst?

treasures

speaking of scars until they become treasures

eucalyptus pods

she licks the wounds of logistics
she lays her hope like eucalyptus pods
scattered, sharp chest open wide
mouth eats you whole
wonder wild for a moment, won't you?
what is this wonderful life for,
if not the dapple of sour or sweet grass
between the passing of roads
damp earth on the balls of our feet
two hearts reaching through distance
choosing longing is its own wealth

good girl belonging

i will not be right
to the hungry good girl:
the wolf is in your heart guzzling
greedy without the pack
wild in invisibility
be seen, beloved.

we are not nice starved, costumed
tell me about the hungry animal

let me see, anyway.

bare the fire that comes from witness
some will shrink, some may bare teeth
count the daggers and think of me

and then- what of the parts that soften?
oh could this part be unlovable?
only from one view, dear one

and I will face my wrong
wear the mess proud
clean it up when I can

oh could this part be unlovable?

i will not be right

i will not be right
i tell this to the me that knows it all
i echo I know nothing
philosopher's quote sends Control writhing

i am writhing, withered, wondering
oh what will they think!

collection of myself

tonight I gather myself dark blue
sharp red at some joints
calling in vertebral lullabies
floating night
the cold gathers around my ankles
perhaps without the kiss of warmth tomorrow
sometimes offers
and in the gathering
an uncovering
a pulling in of the parts
what lies within the collection of myself?
today a crooked throat
bending towards this beam of heart
and I can't quite find the light
while knowing morning is coming
(something lost)

mother maiden us

this is a conversation.

what might you find
amongst the rainbow tiles and sandy socks?
the crusty dish, spilled water, overturned car,
an empty basket,
a bowl of blueberries?
what of the crumbs between the cushions,
the fur collecting on the blankets,
the cascade of books and blocks?
the cacophony of belongings
in the bellowing silence of the neighborhood yard
i find Agony and I call her crazy
with bare feet on frozen street
with the dewy grass ice nearly between my rooting toes
with my heart reaching through my fingers
i want to talk of longing
like the maple tree,
shifting hematoma purple yellow
sticky like connective tissue to bone
crackle too
the wisp wasp of yearn swirling
and I keep not getting met
keep not quite dropping these old leaves

keep holding to some old vision...

so when you meet my sacred rage
i mean to tell you I am left wanting and needing
aching
the boundary-less boundary maker of my children
chosen from this body but not for this life
how can I love it all
what is the poem in the face of destruction?
just a twinkling truth in despair's pit
the sharp voice of truth
like the quiet light in a sea of dark

animal body overwhelm
cortex override

we've made a mess. how will we clean it up?
this is the labor of mothers.

and who will mother us?
this sprawling wide earth
this single cellular star
we beg tomorrow to tend to yesterday
where is our connection to ground?
to that which we capitalize into purpose
formless function

how do we call attention to glaring obvious?
chasms
today it's with a smile and a seeing

oh how I wish we could Know.

not at all

sometimes
I am detail hiding
seed spilling a quiet affair
distilled center radiating
precious silent still
perhaps then it's easiest
to count my tips, points, edges
the way form catches light
slanted, true
the way I am what you see and yet not at all
dimensions below
encased in light
& when we are sharp teeth
i try to love us anyway
gathering the fallen parts
pressing them to cheek like sunshine
before sliding them under soils surface
to continue making blooms

sun curve

drawn to straight lines?
contemplate the curve of the sun
reaching through the window
created by earth's tendril
turn your cheek to the arch of a hill
the slope of the mountain
your body spirals like the earth
like the vine around the budding sunflower
your spine?
she can move in infinities
oscillate freely and frequently
dear one
your birth right is a rippling form
swaying like the sea & river
shaping wherever you shift

sister, remember?

oh, sister
i forgot that i am but blood and heart
and now that i've remembered

i think i'll dance

wildlings

We are in a car until the bottom drops out, we free fall
states, homes, years, selves. Our roots twist dark and
deep through layers of multi hued mud, we are teeth and
rage, we are open wide space, we are authority cowering,
we are what was transmuting. And the spiral ever furls,
the symmetry seeps through time as she is passing, what
was continues to be as we mind our path. Mess makers,
wildlings, wide open feelers. Unsafe and real, secure and
bound. Sometimes souls get tied up the same, though fall
from greatly different stories. You as you, me as me, us as
us. I release.

footpath

sweet little god how you've grown
and how I forgot
how you help me remember
clean as the river
everything else is noise

precious ones,
near here's a foot path over a stream
tread light
the felled log sinks
without awareness, sputtering mud

and when we are muddied
will we giggle or recoil?

oh beloved
getting back to soft
takes effort, courage!

until it doesn't

and then again we are free

9 789369 549993